```
JB                    484769
Bea                    12.95
(Beatles)
Loewen
Beatles
```

DATE DUE			

GREAT RIVER REGIONAL LIBRARY

St. Cloud, Minnesota   56301

PROFILES · IN · MUSIC
The Beatles

LIBRARY OF CONGRESS CATALOGING-IN-PUBLICATION DATA

Loewen, Nancy, 1964-
   Beatles / by Nancy Loewen.
     p. cm. -- (Profiles in music)
   Includes index.
   Summary: Describes how the four boys from Liverpool achieved phenomenal success as the Beatles, their growth as musicians, the pressures of international fame, and their breakup in 1970.
   ISBN 0-86592-610-7
   1. Beatles--Juvenile literature. 2. Rock musicians--England--Biography--Juvenile literature. [1. Beatles. 2. Musicians. 3. Rock music.] I. Title. II. Series: Loewen, Nancy, 1964- Profiles in music.
ML3930.B39L6 1989
782.42166'092'2--dc20   89-33251
[B]   CIP
                                            AC MN

© 1989 Rourke Enterprises, Inc.

All rights reserved. No part of this book may be reproduced or utilized in any form or by any means, electronic or mechanical, including photocopying, recording or by any information storage and retrieval system without permission in writing from the publisher.

PROFILES · IN · MUSIC
The Beatles

TEXT BY
NANCY LOEWEN

DESIGN & PRODUCTION BY
MARK E. AHLSTROM
(The Bookworks)

ROURKE ENTERPRISES, INC.
Vero Beach, FL 32964
U.S.A.

484769

4226031

THE BEATLES

TABLE OF CONTENTS

Introduction	6
Chapter 1: Growing Up in Liverpool	11
Chapter 2: The Quarry Men	23
Chapter 3: Best Band in Liverpool	35
Chapter 4: National Success	47
Chapter 5: Digging the Beatles	61
Chapter 6: The Price of Success	75
Chapter 7: Sign of the Times	85
Chapter 8: Separate Lives	101
Glossary	108-109
Index	110
Listening Choices	111

CREDITS

PHOTOS:

John Zimmerman/FPG International .... cover photo, 4
Photoworld/FPG 22, 34, 57, 58, 59, 60, 74, 100, 107
FPG International 46

TYPESETTING AND LAYOUT: THE FINAL WORD
PRINTING: WORZALLA PUBLISHING CO.

The Beatles: Fab Four

A train pulls out of Penn Station in New York City. It makes its way to Washington, D.C., through thickly falling snow. Despite the bad weather, crowds of teenagers line the platforms at every station along the way. They clutch eagerly at signs and cameras. What a thrill it would be to get a glimpse of the four young men from England!

It is February 11, 1964, and the Beatles are about to appear in concert for the very first time in the United States.

The timing of this exciting event couldn't be better. The Beatles' single, "I Want to Hold Your Hand," is at the top of the charts. Their *Meet the Beatles* album is being rushed to the stores as fast as it can be pressed. With their "mop top" hair and catchy rock 'n' roll, the Beatles have already won the heart of the nation.

The train carrying John Lennon, Paul McCartney, George Harrison, and Ringo Starr comes to a stop at Union Station in Washington, D.C. Three thousand fans have already gathered there, screaming and crying at the thought of the Beatles being near. Outside the Washington Coliseum, where the Beatles will soon be performing, the mob scene is even worse.

The historic concert becomes a reality at 8:31 p.m. Wearing their trademark suits and ties, the Beatles take the stage. The roar of more than 8,000 fans is so loud that the Beatles can hardly hear themselves sing—but sing they do. With Ringo on the drums and the others playing guitars, the Beatles go through "Please Please Me," "I Want to Hold Your Hand," "Twist and Shout," and many others.

Cheering fans pelt the stage with jelly beans, George's favorite candy. They throw flashbulbs, too, which create tiny explosions when they hit the stage. Through it all, the Beatles keep smiling and singing.

The four kids from Liverpool have done all right.

• • •

• • •

It all started in the mid-1950's, when four teenage boys from Liverpool, England, fell in love with rock 'n' roll. Although they didn't know one another at the time, they had a lot in common. They were smart, but not all that interested in school. They had no formal musical training. Their families were far from rich. Yet when they got together, something magical happened. The team of John Lennon, Paul McCartney, George Harrison, and Ringo Starr became one of the most popular music groups ever.

As a symbol of the 1960's, the Beatles both shaped and reflected their culture. Fans watched their every move as the Beatles took their generation through long hair, flowered clothing, drugs, and Eastern religions. The Beatles' most lasting influence, however, is undoubtedly their music itself.

Elvis Presley, Little Richard, and Chuck Berry shook up the world with that thing called rock 'n' roll. The Beatles explored the many possibilities within the music itself. They proved that rock could include everything from orchestras to Indian sitars. It could be sweetly simple or distorted and harsh.

Until the Beatles conquered America in 1964, few Americans cared about British bands. The Beatles changed all that. Their popularity sparked what is called the "British Invasion." Americans couldn't get enough of bands like the Animals, the Kinks, and the Rolling Stones. The United States and Great Britain were now firm allies in music, as well as in politics.

When the Beatles broke up in 1970, their fans were very upset. For years, many people hoped that someday the "Fab Four" would get back together. That dream came to a violent end on December 8, 1980, when John Lennon was shot to death by a mentally disturbed fan in New York City.

Yet the music created by this talented group will never be forgotten. More than two decades after the Beatles' heyday, their songs are played by radio stations around the world. People still buy Beatles' albums, especially now that compact discs have made sound quality better than ever before. Songs like "Eleanor Rigby," "Yesterday," and "Revolution" are enjoyed by today's teenagers nearly as much as by their parents.

The phenomenon of the Beatles may never be completely understood. Perhaps it doesn't need to be. It's enough that four young men made it happen. As John Lennon once said, "We gave everything for 10 years. We gave **ourselves**." For that, the music world will always be grateful.

CHAPTER 1: GROWING UP IN LIVERPOOL

"The guitar's all very well, John, but you'll never make a living out of it."

—Aunt Mimi to John Lennon

The Setting

The city of Liverpool is located on the northwest coast of England, where the Mersey River empties into the Irish Sea. Along the river banks are more than 600 acres of ship docks. During World War II, Liverpool's location made the city a major supply line —and a prime target for Hitler's bombs. "A man could walk across the river Mersey on the hulls of sunken ships," local people grimly joked.

Liverpool was never a very glamorous city. But it did have something other towns didn't: an active musical scene. There were always plenty of local bands playing in coffee bars and dance halls. Young people from Liverpool especially liked American music, brought over by visiting American sailors. When rock music was born in the 1950's, Liverpool's teenagers went mad for American singers like Bill Haley and the Comets, Little Richard, and of course, Elvis Presley.

Another trend made its mark in Liverpool at about the same time. Early in 1956, Lonnie Donegan had a number-one hit with the song,

"Rock Island Line." But it wasn't just another top-selling record. It started a whole new fad in music, called "skiffle."

Skiffle was simple jazz or folk music played by a group. What made it unique was that some—or all—of the players used homemade or low-cost instruments. These included kitchen washboards, tin cans, and kazoos. Many skiffle groups also had at least one person playing the guitar. Thanks to Elvis Presley, the guitar was now a very popular instrument.

Teenagers liked to dance to the catchy rhythms of skiffle. They liked to play it even more. Thousands of quickly formed skiffle groups sprang up all over England.

One of those new groups was led by a 16-year-old named John Lennon.

John Lennon

John Lennon was born in Liverpool on October 9, 1940, to the sounds of Nazi bombing. His father, Fred Lennon, was away at sea when he was born.

Except for a brief visit when John was five years old, Fred Lennon never came back.

John's mother, Julia, was a happy, carefree woman. She loved to laugh and joke. But she knew that she wasn't any better at being a parent than Fred was. When John was still very young, he was sent to live with Julia's sister, Mimi, and her husband. Mimi and George Smith lived in the suburb of Woolton. Julia lived nearby, though, and sometimes surprised her son with a visit.

Growing up, John was usually bored with school, even though he had learned to read before he was five years old. In study hall, he'd draw cruel—but funny—cartoons of his teachers and classmates. After school he and his friends would sometimes shoplift candy or cigarettes. His uncle George died when John was 12. After that, John became even more of a rebel.

Then, in 1956, 16-year-old John Lennon discovered rock 'n' roll.

At that time it wasn't possible to just turn on the radio and listen to rock music. Unlike the United States, Britain had no commercial radio stations. Instead, the British Broadcasting Corporation (BBC) controlled three stations—one for classical music, one for "light" music, and one for news. None of the stations played rock 'n' roll.

There were only two ways for Liverpool teenagers to hear American rock. One was from the records brought into the city by young men working on the docks. The other was to listen to the "English Service" program on Radio Luxembourg. Radio Luxembourg was a privately owned station in Belgium. It had a signal strong enough to reach England and most of central Europe.

Every night at 8 o'clock, John would sit in his bedroom and listen to his cheap, crackling radio. This was where he heard Elvis Presley's first big hit, "Heartbreak Hotel." John was impressed with the song—and how! "From then on, I never got a minute's peace," recalled Mimi. "It was Elvis Presley, Elvis Presley, Elvis Presley."

Then the skiffle craze hit, and John decided he just **had** to have a guitar. Aunt Mimi gave in and bought him one. With his precious guitar in hand,

John practiced until his fingers bled. Mimi was glad to see John show an interest in something besides making trouble. Still, she was concerned about his future. "The guitar's all very well, John, but you'll never make a living at it," she told him.

Once he had mastered the basics, John formed a skiffle group with a buddy of his, Pete Shotton. They called themselves the Quarry Men because they both went to Quarry Bank High School. Other classmates joined the group, too, but they came and went. That's how most skiffle groups worked. The main goal was just to have fun.

The Quarry Men played mostly at friends' parties. They also competed in the skiffle contests that were always being held at small dance halls. The Quarry Men didn't do very well in the contests, though. One group in particular always beat them. That group featured a midget named Nicky Cuff— who actually stood on his homemade bass while he played it!

Paul McCartney

On June 18, 1942, a big-eyed baby son was born to Mary and Jim McCartney. They named him James Paul, but everyone just called him Paul. The boy was a charmer from the start. He could usually manage to get his own way—without making it seem too obvious. In school, he did well without even really trying.

Paul McCartney was the only Beatle born into a musical family. Years earlier, his father had been the leader of the Jim Mac Jazz Band. Paul would often listen to his dad play the piano in the living room, and learned to play a little himself. Paul played the trumpet, too, but he was more interested in singing. He often sang to himself in bed, before going to sleep. Sometimes his family would listen at the bottom of the stairs.

When Paul was 14 years old, his mother died of cancer. The family—which also included Paul's younger brother, Michael—was shattered.

As Paul adjusted to life without his mother, music became even more important to him. Jim

McCartney sensed this. Somehow, he managed to scrape up enough money for the guitar Paul wanted so badly.

At first Paul couldn't play the instrument very well, no matter how hard he tried. Something just wasn't quite right. Then he discovered that when it came to playing guitar, he was left-handed! He decided to reverse the guitar strings, and that did the trick.

George Harrison

George Harrison was born on February 25, 1943, to Harry and Louise Harrison. Besides being the youngest Beatle, George was also the baby of his family. He got a lot of attention from his two older brothers and an older sister. Yet, even as a child, he was always very independent.

To his classmates, George was known as the kid whose dad drove the pale green buses they all took to school. At first, George did well in school. As he grew older, though, he became bored with his classes and began to dislike the school routines.

His studies suffered even more when Lonnie Donegan burst onto the musical scene. Around this time, George's mother started noticing a strange thing. In the pockets of George's pants were scraps of paper with guitars drawn on them. It wasn't hard to figure out what was on George's mind!

When George asked his mother for money to buy a used guitar from a schoolmate, Louise Harrison agreed. Sometimes she even sat up with him at night as he practiced. Unlike the other Beatles, playing the guitar wasn't easy for George. He had to struggle to make his fingers move smoothly and firmly over the strings.

Slowly, his efforts paid off. As his confidence increased, his guitar playing got better and better. His new-found skills even won him a friend—an older kid on his school bus named Paul McCartney.

Ringo Starr

Ringo Starr—whose real name is Richard Starkey—was born one month late on July 7, 1940, during a heavy bombing raid. Like John Lennon, he never got to know his father very well. Richard and Elsie Starkey divorced when Ringo was very young, and he lived with his mother. Elsie worked as a bar maid in order to make ends meet. She and Ringo lived in the "Dingle," one of the roughest sections of Liverpool.

When Ringo was six years old, he suffered a burst appendix. Surgeons quickly operated on him. They saved his life, but the little boy was in a coma for many weeks. By the time he was well enough to go back to school, he'd already missed a full year. He never quite caught up with his classmates.

Ringo's health problems weren't over yet. When he was 13, a simple cold turned into a lung disease called pleurisy. This time he was in a children's hospital for two years. By the time he was released, he was no longer required to attend school, so he quit.

When the skiffle craze hit in 1956, the ever-cheerful Ringo was working at a local engineering firm. He and a co-worker formed their own group, often playing for the other workers during their lunch hour. Ringo mostly played the drums.

Skiffle soon fell by the wayside, but Ringo kept getting better on the drums. By 1959 he was a professional drummer with Rory Storm and the Hurricanes. This was the hottest band in Liverpool at the time. It was while playing with this band that Richard Starkey became Ringo Starr. The guys in the group called him "Ringo" for the simple reason that he always wore a lot of rings. They shortened his last name to "Starr" because they wanted to announce his drum solo with the dramatic words, "It's Starr Time!"

The Beatles started their musical careers playing in "skiffle" bands. When the skiffle craze ended, the Beatles just kept going!

CHAPTER 2: THE QUARRY MEN

"Was it better to have a guy who was better than the people I had in, obviously, or not? To make the group stronger or to let me be stronger?"

—John Lennon on inviting Paul to join the Quarry Men

Lennon & McCartney Team Up

Every summer, St. Peter's Parish Church in Woolton held a fête, or festival, for the neighborhood. The activities included a parade, carnival, bake sale, music, and dance. Providing the music for 1957's fête was a skiffle group called the Quarry Men, led by John Lennon.

In the crowd that day was a chubby-cheeked 15-year-old named Paul McCartney. His main reason for coming to the fête didn't have anything to do with music. He just wanted to meet girls! But as he watched the Quarry Men play on the makeshift stage behind the church, something about John Lennon got his attention.

Later in the afternoon, the two young musicians met each other for the first time. A classmate of Paul's introduced him to the group as the Quarry Men set up their instruments for the evening dance.

Grabbing a guitar, Paul played some Eddie Cochran songs for them. The group, especially John, was impressed. Paul was good. And he even knew all the words! This was a big advantage, since song lyrics weren't printed out in those days. John often made up the words as he went along.

There was one other skill Paul McCartney could offer the group. He knew how to tune a guitar. None of the Quarry Men had mastered that important job yet. Whenever his guitar needed tuning, John had to take it to a local music shop!

After he met Paul, John Lennon had a lot of thinking to do. "Was it better to have a guy who was better than the people I had in, obviously, or not? To make the group stronger or to let me be stronger?" John recounted in a later interview. "That decision was to let Paul in and make the group stronger."

A couple of weeks later, Paul was riding his bike when he came across Quarry Man Pete Shotton. "Hey!" Pete called. "They say they'd quite like to have you in the band, if you'd like to join."

Breathlessly, Paul replied, "That'd be great!"

Getting Better All the Time

Around the time Paul joined the Quarry Men, skiffle was on its way out. Performances for the group were few and far between. But that didn't keep Paul and John—who'd quickly become good friends—from practicing their guitars and singing together. In order to see the new chords Paul showed him, John even broke down and wore the glasses he hated so much.

The first time Paul McCartney played with the group was an October performance at the New Clubmoor Hall. It didn't go quite as he had hoped. "I had this big solo and it came to my bit and I blew it," Paul remembered. "Sticky fingers, you know. I couldn't play at all and I got terribly embarrassed. So I goofed that one terribly, and so from then on I was on rhythm guitar. Blown out on lead!"

Early in 1958, Paul made a suggestion to the group. His buddy, George Harrison, was a talented guitar player. Why not ask him to join the Quarry Men, too? John wasn't so sure. True, George was good. But he was barely 15 years old! To 17-year-old John, George was just a kid.

George Harrison was never formally asked to join the Quarry Men. But he started hanging around with them, and often sat in for other guitarists when they couldn't make it. Gradually, the others started thinking of him as part of the group.

Julia

A lot of changes were taking place in the lives of the Quarry Men. John Lennon had finished high school in July, 1957, with a dismal record. Although he wasn't too concerned about his future, Aunt Mimi was. She spent a lot of time talking to John's principal about her nephew's plans.

Finally, by pulling a few strings, the principal managed to get John a spot in the Liverpool College of Art. In his request, the principal wrote, "John is not beyond redemption and could possibly turn out to be a fairly responsible adult who might go far."

At first, John was excited about being an art student. But it didn't take long before boredom set in once more. He thought art school would give him a chance to be creative. Instead, it just seemed like rules, rules, rules.

One day, Paul happened to show John a song he'd written himself. Nothing was the same after that. Until then, John had just played around with song lyrics—often forgetting them during performances. Now he started to pay more attention to his own musical ideas. The two teenagers entered into a friendly competition, each writing his own songs. But they often joined forces and worked together, too. In their first year, they wrote more than 100 songs!

From the very beginning, the boys' song-writing styles balanced each other out. Paul's work was usually sweet and sentimental. John's work had more of a cynical edge. Later, that difference would stand out even more.

Around this time, John began spending more time with his mother, Julia. More like a friend than a parent, she was very enthusiastic about

John's group. She even knew the words to most of the Quarry Men songs. Sadly, that relationship never had a chance to develop. One summer evening in July 1958, Julia was walking to the bus stop when she was hit by a car. She died instantly.

On the surface, John Lennon took on the role of "tough guy." He didn't show very much emotion about his mother's death. People didn't expect him to. After all, his mother hadn't raised him. But at the art college, he spent many hours by himself, just looking out the window at the top of the rear stairwell. Once a friend noticed that he was crying. "It was the worst thing that ever happened to me," John Lennon said later about his mother's death.

Rocking the Casbah

For the next year or so, the Quarry Men didn't perform very much. It looked like the group was through. Then they got a steady job at the Casbah Coffee Club, and their playing days started up again.

The Casbah was operated by Mona Best and her two teenage sons. By adding bench seats and a counter, they had converted the big basement in their home into a real club. Mona herself sold the coffee, snacks, and soft drinks to the dozens of kids who hung out there.

From August to October 1959, the Quarry Men played the Casbah every Saturday night. Their performances got better and better with regular playing. Then they had an argument with Mona Best and walked out. Soon, however, their connection with the club would come in handy.

Early in 1960, the Quarry Men added a new member named Stuart Sutcliffe. Stu was a friend of John's from art school. He was a very gifted painter, and an intellectual besides. He and John Lennon could talk for hours about their ideas on art, literature, and life in general.

With his dark hair and pale face, people said Stu looked like Hollywood star James Dean. Stu made the most of his image—wearing tight jeans, pink shirts, and dark glasses. Being in a band, he thought, would be the finishing touch.

When Stu sold one of his paintings at an important art exhibit, he knew just what to do with the money. Instead of paying off his debts or buying art supplies, he spent the money on a bass guitar and joined the Quarry Men. But he never really mastered the instrument. Sometimes he even stood with his back to the audience, hoping they wouldn't catch on to his lack of skill. For the most part, they didn't.

Growing Pains

During their free evenings and lunch hours, the Quarry Men would often go to the Jacaranda Coffee Club. The Jac, as they called it, was run by a man named Allan Williams. He would let the boys sit there for hours, even when all they could afford to buy was a cup of coffee.

Allan Williams was very much tuned into the band scene in Liverpool. It was through him that the Quarry Men got their first real break: backing up singer Johnny Gentle on a nine-day tour of Scotland.

The Quarry Men were thrilled when they got the news. They pictured a glamorous trip, with fame and fortune soon to follow. But they couldn't have been more wrong. The tour was just a series of one-night stands in run-down dance halls. When they came home, they were tired, hungry—and a little wiser.

Back in Liverpool, Allan Williams booked the group all over town. Often they played in rough neighborhoods, where they had to watch out for the destructive "Teddy Boys." The Teds wore narrow trousers, pointed boots, bright shirts, and long hair piled high on their heads. The Quarry Men themselves liked to dress like that, to the great dismay of their families. But they were no match for the real Teddy Boys, who were older, stronger, and often very violent.

During one Quarry Men performance in a crowded hall, a group of Teds booted a 16-year-old boy to death. Another time, the Teds focused on Stu for some reason. They waited for him outside the dance hall. When he came out, they threw him to the ground and kicked him in the head. Luckily,

John Lennon was able to help Stu get away. Though it took a long time for Stu's head to stop bleeding, he refused to see a doctor.

As the group learned more and more about what it meant to be a real rock band, they went through quite a few name changes. Since their favorite group at the time was Buddy Holly and the Crickets, they decided on an "insect" theme. For a while, they were the Beatals. Then they decided on the Silver Beetles, followed by the Silver Beatles. Finally, in August 1960, they settled on the Beatles. This time the name stuck.

By the early 1960's, the Beatles had plenty of devoted fans in their hometown of Liverpool. Soon they would have fans around the world! Standing from left to right are: Paul McCartney, George Harrison, John Lennon, and Ringo Starr.

CHAPTER 3
BEST BAND IN LIVERPOOL

"It was pretty much of an eye-opener, to go down into this darkened, dank, smoky cellar in the middle of the day, and to see crowds and crowds of kids watching these four young men on stage."

—Brian Epstein on seeing the Beatles play the Cavern Club

"Making Show" in Hamburg

The band, now made up of John, Paul, George, and Stu, soon got another taste of life outside Liverpool. Working through Allan Williams, they were hired for an engagement in Hamburg, West Germany. There was only one problem. They still didn't have a permanent drummer.

By chance they wandered back into the Casbah Club one night—and there was 18-year-old Pete Best with a brand-new set of drums. Pete agreed to become a Beatle, and their problem was solved. In late summer of 1960, the group took off for Hamburg.

Because of its active night life, Hamburg was often referred to as "the Las Vegas of Europe." In the Reeperbahn, or red-light district, there was always a lot happening—from drinking and dancing to crime, drugs, and prostitution. In the middle of it all were the Beatles, as well as several other Liverpool bands.

The Beatles started out by playing the Indra

Club, a small, grimy place that used to be a strip joint. After about six weeks, the Indra was shut down. The Beatles were next sent to the Kaiserkeller, which was bigger and a bit more plush than the Indra.

The Hamburg audiences liked to see lively bands. At first, the Beatles weren't used to this. They usually didn't move around very much while performing. Now, encouraged by calls of *"mach shau!"* (make show), they began to loosen up. All the "pep pills" and beer they were consuming may have helped with that, too.

At the Kaiserkeller, the group split shifts with another Liverpool band, Rory Storm and the Hurricanes. Drumming for that group was none other than Ringo Starr.

The two bands had a lot of fun together. Once they started a contest to see which band could be the first to break through the Kaiserkeller's old, rotting stage. Rory Storm finally managed it, crashing through in the middle of "Blue Suede Shoes." The owner was furious.

Around this time, a new—and much nicer—

club opened nearby. Whenever they had the chance, the Beatles would run over to the Top Ten Club, run by Peter Eckhorn. Sometimes they even played there, violating their Kaiserkeller contract.

Then everything came crashing down. The police discovered that George Harrison, at 17, was still a minor. Past midnight, his very presence in the Reeperbahn was illegal. Alone and scared, George was put on a train back to Liverpool.

A few days later, Paul McCartney and Pete Best were accused of setting fire to a moldy tapestry in their filthy living quarters. Although no major damage was done, they were ordered out of town. John Lennon and Stu Sutcliffe soon followed.

"My Bonnie Lies Over the Ocean"

Back home in Liverpool, the Beatles were tired and discouraged. A couple of weeks passed before they bothered to get in touch with one another. Finally, a week before Christmas, they gave their first post-Hamburg performance to a full house at the Casbah Club.

During the months they'd been in Hamburg, the Beatles had improved a great deal. More than 500 hours of playing had turned the former skiffle band into genuine rock 'n' rollers. Liverpool audiences were quick to respond to the change. They tried to get as close as they could to the charismatic performers. On a small scale, Beatlemania had begun!

From January to March 1961, the Beatles had so many bookings that they had to hire someone just to drive them around. Neil Aspinall, a friend of Pete Best's, soon became their permanent road manager.

Despite their new-found popularity in their hometown, the Beatles weren't through with Hamburg yet. What they really wanted was to play for Pete Eckhorn at the Top Ten Club. This wouldn't be easy. Because of the incident with the tapestry, Paul and Pete needed permission from West Germany's Foreign Department just to enter the country. George Harrison's problem had been solved—he'd turned 18—but they all needed to get legal working permits this time.

Finally, with Eckhorn's help, everything was arranged. By the end of March, the Beatles were once more enjoying the intense Hamburg nightlife. They even had a small following ready to welcome them back.

One of their Hamburg fans was a young woman named Astrid Kirchherr. Actually, she was much more than a fan—she and Stu had gotten engaged during the Beatles' first visit to Hamburg. Astrid was a gifted art student and photographer with a unique sense of style.

Thanks to Astrid, the Beatles' "look" underwent a few changes. One day she sat Stu down, brushed his hair over his forehead, and cut it into bowl-shaped bangs. The Beatles couldn't help snickering when they saw Stu's new cut. Gradually, though, they came to like it. One by one, they had their hair cut the same soon-to-be-famous way.

Being with Astrid made Stu eager to get back to his true talent: painting. He enrolled in a Hamburg art college, and began spending less time with the band. Paul took over his spot on bass guitar, and the Beatles became a four-man band.

Besides their regular playing at the Top Ten Club, the Beatles also played backup for a popular 20-year-old British singer named Tony Sheridan. This turned out to be a lucky break for the group. When Tony made a record for Polydor Records, the Beatles were invited to be his backup band.

One of the songs they recorded was a rocked-up version of "My Bonnie Lies Over the Ocean." It was released as a single, credited to Tony Sheridan and the "Beat Brothers." Polydor thought the word "Beatle" sounded too much like an obscene German word!

Sweating It Out in the Cavern Club

When the Beatles returned to Liverpool in August 1961, they were more in demand than ever. The Cavern Club was where they played the most. In fact, in the next two years they would perform there nearly 300 times.

The Cavern Club was very popular among rock fans, in spite of the conditions that gave the club its name—or maybe because of them. It was located beneath a former warehouse. The lighting was poor. There were no tables or carpets. Worst of all, there was no ventilation system.

Yet, when the Beatles played there, those things didn't seem to matter. Hundreds of people jammed into the club. It didn't take long before everyone was sweating. Condensation ran down the walls. Steam hung in the air. Sometimes the Beatles themselves were surrounded by such a wet vapor they were at risk of being electrocuted!

By now, there was no question about it—the Beatles were something special. They were the number-one group in Liverpool. They had made a record. They had more gigs than they knew what to do with. Yet even as their local fans cheered, the group was starting to feel a little let down. Where could they go from here?

The man who would answer that question walked down the 18 stone steps to the Cavern Club on November 9, 1961. His name was Brian Epstein.

Manage Us!

At 27 years of age, Brian Epstein was the manager of the very successful Liverpool branch of North End Music Stores (NEMS). There had recently been several requests for the German-released "My Bonnie Lies Over the Ocean." Brian was told that the "Beat Brothers" were really Liverpool's own Beatles. Then he learned that they were regulars at the Cavern Club, not more than 200 yards from his store.

Curious, Brian decided to visit the Cavern Club during a lunchtime performance. He wanted to see this popular Liverpool group for himself.

With his elegant suit and a briefcase tucked under his arm, Brian Epstein was hardly the typical Cavern patron. But he was glad he went.

"It was pretty much of an eye-opener, to go down into this darkened, dank, smoky cellar in the middle of the day, and to see crowds and crowds of kids watching these four young men on stage," he recounted later in a radio interview.

"They were rather scruffily dressed—black

leather jackets and jeans, long hair of course," he continued. "And they had a rather untidy stage presentation, not terribly aware, and not caring very much, what they looked like. I think they cared more, even then, for what they sounded like...I immediately liked what I heard."

Brian Epstein came to the Cavern often after that. There was just something about the Beatles that fascinated him. Then he had a wild idea. What if he were to become the group's manager and promoter? With his help, maybe the Beatles could become stars!

Although his family and business associates thought he was crazy, Brian went ahead with his plans. Meetings were set up between the Beatles and their would-be manager. By promising them a deal with a major recording company and a way out of Liverpool, Brian said the magic words. "Right, then, Brian," John Lennon blurted out excitedly. "Manage us." The rest of the band eagerly agreed.

With Brian a part of the team, the Beatles began to make some changes. Eating, drinking, or smoking on stage might be all right at the Cavern Club, but it wouldn't do in other places, Brian insisted. From then on, the Beatles were to know exactly which songs they'd be singing, and in which order. And instead of the leather and denim they'd been wearing all along, the Beatles would wear identical suits—and ties.

"No way!" they all protested when they heard that last one, but they soon gave in. Anything was worth a try.

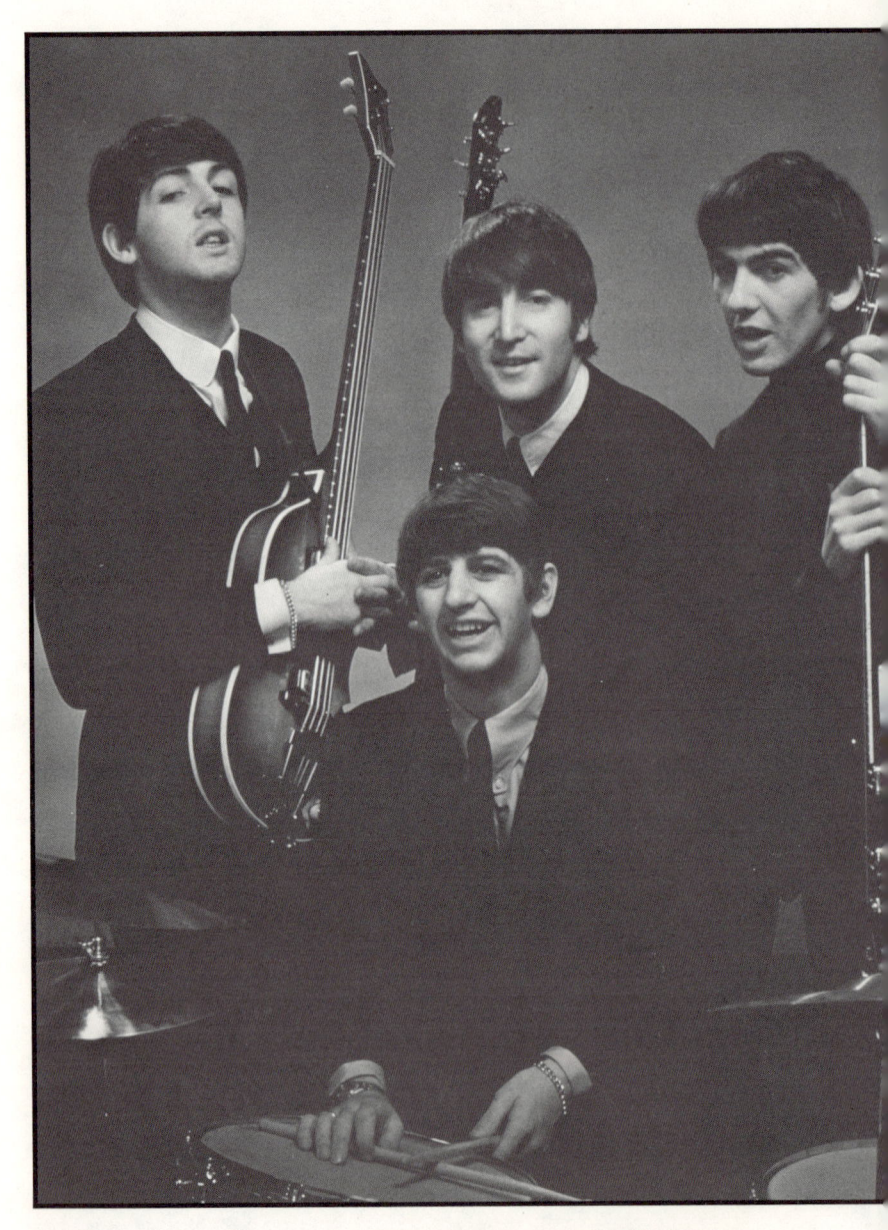

In their early days, the Beatles spent a great deal of time playing to crowded clubs in Hamburg, West Germany. They quickly became charismatic performers.

CHAPTER 4
NATIONAL SUCCESS

"Gentlemen, you have just recorded your first Number One."

—Producer George Martin after the recording of "Please Please Me"

Losing
a Friend

On a snowy New Year's Day in 1962, the Beatles auditioned with Decca Records in London. After playing for so long in places like the Cavern Club, the studio atmosphere threw them off. Their usual energy was missing as they sang to the blank-faced men behind the glass window of the control room.

Still, as they waited to hear Decca's decision, they were hopeful—and with good reason. "My Bonnie Lies Over the Ocean" had been released in England. They'd made their radio debut on the BBC program, "Teenagers' Turn." And a popularity poll had officially dubbed them the number-one group in Liverpool.

Two months passed before they received Decca's reply. It was a very firm "no."

The Beatles were terribly disappointed when they got the bad news. Brian Epstein was furious. He stormed over to the Decca offices to get some answers. "The Beatles won't go, Mr. Epstein," was all the management would say. "We know these things."

Brian couldn't believe what he was hearing. "I am completely confident that one day they will be bigger than Elvis Presley!" he said in his haughtiest voice. The Decca people just smiled to themselves. That's what all the managers said.

At last, Brian realized that getting the Beatles a contract would not be as easy as he had thought. During the next few months, he made dozens of phone calls. He wrote letter after letter. He paid many visits to recording executives. But the answer was always the same—"not interested."

In April, glad to get away from their worries in Liverpool, the Beatles went back to Hamburg. This time they were to headline at the Star Club, a new nightclub that was much bigger than any of the other places where they'd performed.

Just before they left, they received two telegrams from Astrid. The first one said that Stu Sutcliffe was very ill. The second one said that he had died.

For a long time, Stu had been fighting terrible

headaches. He'd gotten pale and thin. Though he had all the symptoms of a brain tumor, nothing had shown up on his X-rays. After his death, however, doctors finally discovered a tiny tumor. Right above it was a small dent in the skull—about the same size as the steel tip of a Teddy Boy's boot. Stu's death was probably caused that night in 1960, when he was beaten up after playing a show in Liverpool.

It was hard to believe that Stu could be dead at the age of 21.

A Foot in the Door

Trying to put their grief behind them, the Beatles threw themselves into the unreal nightlife of the Reeperbahn like never before. The Star Club was a good place in which to forget the rest of the world. Sometimes as many as 18,000 people would come and go during the course of an evening! The Beatles were a big hit, but they weren't the only attraction at the club. A lot of folks came to see the women mud wrestlers, too.

While the Beatles "made show" at the Star Club, Brian Epstein worked harder than ever to get them a recording contract. On one of his trips to London, he had the Beatles' demo tape transferred to a black acetate disc. He hoped this would impress the record executives.

But it was the music itself that impressed the engineer who made the disc. In a fateful series of events, the engineer referred Brian to the director of a song-publishing business. In turn, that director suggested Brian try EMI's Parlophone label.

EMI was a British corporation that made electronic equipment. It controlled several recording labels as well. Brian Epstein and the Beatles had already been turned down by two EMI labels, Columbia and HMV. But they hadn't approached Parlophone yet. Parlophone was a smaller label, featuring mostly comedy and novelty albums. It was run by a man named George Martin.

Something must have clicked between Brian and George Martin. The Beatles could hardly believe it when they read the telegram Brian sent.

"Congratulations boys. EMI requests recording session. Please rehearse new material," it read.

Starr Time

In early June 1962, the Beatles set foot for the first time in the EMI Abbey Road studios. The studios were located in a quiet, tree-lined residential area in London called St. John's Wood. George Martin listened closely as the Beatles ran through their songs. Although he thought they had potential, he didn't make them an offer right away.

Later in the summer, George came to a decision. The Beatles could have a contract—on the condition that Pete Best be replaced on the drums.

Rather than defend their drummer, the Beatles agreed to replace Pete. At that point, cruel as it was, their hunger for success was far greater than their loyalty. The quiet, reserved Pete had never really "fit in" with the group anyway, they reasoned.

As soon as Brian told the luckless drummer the news, Pete was furious. "It's taken them two years to find out I'm not a good enough drummer?" he shouted and stormed away.

Pete's followers in Liverpool were nearly as upset as he was. Throngs of girls picketed the Cavern Club when the Beatles played there. "Pete is Best!" their signs read. For a few days, Brian needed police escorts just to get to work. His new car was vandalized. The Beatles themselves were provoked into fist fights.

In the meantime, the Beatles had no trouble finding a new drummer. One phone call to Ringo Starr was all it took. They had been friends with Ringo ever since their days playing the Kaiserkeller. Sometimes, when Pete had been sick, Ringo had filled in.

Nothing could have made Ringo happier than to join the popular group. The first thing he did after he got the news was to cut his hair just like the Beatles.

In the middle of all this turmoil, John Lennon quietly married his long-time girlfriend, Cynthia Powell.

"Overnight" Sensation

When the Beatles finally signed with Parlophone, they got more than a contract—they got George Martin as a producer, too. He knew a great deal about the technical aspects of music. Since none of the Beatles could read or write music very well at that time, George was a much-needed addition to the team. He worked very closely with them, never quitting on a song until it was just right.

On October 5, 1962, Parlophone released the Beatles first single, "Love Me Do." It was a simple love song Paul McCartney had written at the age of 16.

As soon as the new song was out, Brian tried to start the ball rolling by ordering 10,000 copies of the record for NEMS. He then organized a letter-writing campaign to Radio Luxembourg and the BBC. The Beatles' fans, friends, family, even the NEMS employees wrote the stations and begged them to play "Love Me Do."

After receiving hundreds of letters, Radio Luxembourg started playing the single. While the Beatles watched in amazement, "Love Me Do" grabbed a foothold on the charts. By mid-December, it was number 17.

Hoping to build on that first success, Parlophone released another single in February 1963. John Lennon had written "Please Please Me" years before, sitting on his Aunt Mimi's pink eyelet bed. Now, at Martin's suggestion, the song was played at a faster tempo. It was good advice.

"Gentlemen, you have just recorded your first number one," said a pleased George Martin at the end of the session.

The Beatles worked hard to make this prediction come true. They stepped up their schedule of performances, playing in small towns and cities all across England. With every day that passed, their audiences seemed to get more enthusiastic. And on March 2, 1963, "Please Please Me" became the Beatles' first number-one hit.

No one has ever been able to explain what happened next.

The Beatles' third single, "From Me to You," was released on April 12. It went to number one just two weeks later. Their fourth single, "She Loves You," rocketed to the top position in August. It was displaced in December—by yet another Beatles hit, "I Want to Hold Your Hand."

The Beatles also released two successful albums. The LP *Please Please Me* hit number one on May 11, where it stayed for 30 weeks. It was knocked out of top position by the Beatles' follow-up album, *With the Beatles*.

In some mysterious way, the Beatles had made a vital connection with the young people of England.

Once the Beatles had their first hit, there was no stopping them. "We thought that everyone would be able to dig at least one of us," John Lennon said, "and that's how it turned out."

When the Beatles made their first appearance on "The Ed Sullivan Show" in 1964, a record-setting 73 million people tuned in. Not even Elvis Presley had attracted such a large audience!

No matter how fast-paced or tiring their schedule was, the Beatles could always manage to put on a good show.

Wherever the Beatles went, crowds of fans were sure to follow. The group is shown here rehearsing for a British television show.

CHAPTER 5: DIGGING THE BEATLES

"None of us has quite grasped what it is all about yet. It's washing over our heads like a huge tidal wave."

—Ringo Starr

No Turning Back

As a result of the Beatles, things were changing in the music world. Thousands of Beatle-imitating bands were formed. New music clubs sprang up all across England. Even the BBC started playing pop music for longer time periods.

Liverpool was now **the** place to be. Record companies beat a hasty path to Liverpool and signed up many of the local bands. Many of the groups did quite well on the charts. The "Mersey sound," as the critics called it, had taken ahold of the nation.

Of course, the Beatles' lives were changing as well. Success had created an even more demanding schedule. That year, besides touring England, they also toured Sweden, Ireland, and Scotland. Along the way, they managed to fit in press interviews, as well as radio and television broadcasts.

For John and Cynthia Lennon, 1963 brought yet another change. Their son, Julian, was born on April 8, 1963. He was named after John's mother.

Although John was on tour when Julian was born, he managed to visit the hospital soon afterwards. Cynthia and the baby were in the hospital's only private room. Actually, the room offered less privacy than they had hoped. A big glass window connected it with the public ward.

Wearing a hat, fake moustache, and dark glasses, John Lennon visited his wife and baby son. But one of the new mothers in the public ward had sharp eyes. "It's 'im! It's one of them, the Beatles!" she cried. Soon patients and nurses alike were gathered at the window, pointing and staring.

That incident was only a taste of things to come. As the year went on, the crowds got bigger and more hysterical with every appearance the Beatles made. Before long, the Beatles were too big for the places that had "made" them. On August 3, 1963, they gave their last performance at the Cavern Club.

The old days were gone forever.

Playing For Royalty

By now, people were paying attention to the Beatles' personalities as well as to their music. Paul was dubbed the cute one, while George was the quiet one. John was the intellectual, and Ringo was the funny one. Of course, those labels hardly told the whole story. But as John once said, "We thought that everyone would be able to dig at least one of us, and that's how it turned out."

Only London, Britain's capital, had yet to be won over by the Beatles. That soon happened. On October 13, the group appeared live on "Val Parnell's Sunday Night at the London Palladium," a popular television variety show. Thousands of fans swarmed into the streets surrounding the Palladium. A record 15 million people sat glued to their television screens. The next day, the Beatles were front-page news. **"BEATLEMANIA"** screamed one descriptive headline.

On November 4, the Beatles performed before Queen Elizabeth and Princess Margaret at the annual Royal Command Performance. The show, held at the Prince of Wales Theater in London, featured various British entertainment acts. Without a doubt, the Beatles were the main attraction at 1963's show. Thousands of excited fans gathered around the theater, held back only by row after row of police.

Less than a year earlier, the Beatles hadn't even had a manager. Now they were drawing more attention than the royal family itself!

Number One in America!

The Beatles were now a household word in England. In late 1963, however, few Americans had even heard of the group. They had a more serious issue to think about. On November 22, 1963, President John F. Kennedy was assassinated in Dallas, Texas. After the shock of his death wore off, the whole nation seemed to be in a state of depression.

For young people, especially, the gloom soon got to be too much. By the end of December, they were more than ready to get excited about something again. The Beatles and their music would create that excitement—and then some.

Only after the Beatles had their fifth "number one" in Britain did Capitol Records, EMI's North American record label, decide to take a chance on the group. "I Want to Hold Your Hand" was scheduled for American release in January 1964. No one expected it to do very well. Up to that time, no British act had been very successful in America. Why should the Beatles be any different?

Then came the first tiny spark of Beatlemania, U.S.A.

A disc jockey at WWDC in Washington, D.C., started playing "I Want To Hold Your Hand." He'd gotten the record from his girlfriend, a flight attendant with a British airline. Almost immediately, the station was flooded with calls. "Where can we get the record?" people wanted to know. "Play it again!"

The WWDC disc jockey then made a tape of the song and sent it to a DJ friend in Chicago. From there the tape went on to St. Louis. In all three cities, the response was the same—the Beatles were a surefire hit.

When Capitol Records found out about the potential blockbuster on their hands, they changed their strategy. As three production plants worked around the clock pressing one million copies of the single, Capitol announced a rush-release the day after Christmas.

On January 16, 1964, the Beatles were performing at the Olympia Theater in Paris, France, when they got some mind-boggling news. "I Want to Hold Your Hand" had jumped from number 43 to number one on the U.S. charts.

The timing couldn't have been better. The United States was the group's next stop.

Out of Their Minds

Even on the plane to New York City, the Beatles could hardly believe they had the number-one song in America. Nearly all the musicians who influenced the Beatles were from America—people like Elvis Presley, Roy Orbison, Carl Perkins, and

Buddy Holly. Rock 'n' roll itself had developed out of American white country music and black rhythm & blues.

"Since America has always had everything, why should we be going over there making money?" Paul McCartney wondered out loud on the plane. "They've got their own groups. What are we going to give them that they don't already have?"

Only the American fans could answer that question—and by now there were plenty of them. When the Beatles' plane touched down at the newly renamed John F. Kennedy Airport in New York City on February 7, 1964, they thought for a moment that someone important must be arriving. Then they realized that the 5,000 screaming, chanting, frenzied teenagers were their new fans!

In a matter of hours, the kids weren't the only ones singing the group's praises. The American press was, too. With their droll humor, the Beatles managed to charm even the most skeptical reporters, just as they had in England. "So this is America," Ringo said to a newsman who asked how the Beatles liked their welcome. "They all seem out of their minds."

The Beatles' first trip to the United States clinched their place in American culture. On February 9, nearly 73 million people tuned in to the "Ed Sullivan Show" to see their live performance. That night, not one hubcap was reported stolen in all of New York City! On February 11, the Beatles gave a sold-out concert at the Washington Coliseum in Washington, D.C. The next day they performed at the prestigious Carnegie Hall in New York City—the first rock concert ever to be performed there. On February 16, they made their second appearance on the "Ed Sullivan Show."

Leaving the United State five days later, they left behind a flurry of Beatles wigs, T-shirts, dolls, pens—even "Beatlenut" ice cream. All of their singles and albums had been re-released, including "My Bonnie Lies Over the Ocean" from those long-ago Hamburg days. Stores were selling them all as fast as shipments came in.

The nation's obsession with the Beatles was easily measured on the record charts. *Billboard's* Hot 100 for the week of April 4, 1964, listed Beatles songs in the top five places—with seven others working their way up! Other British groups, benefiting from the Beatles' popularity, were on the charts as well.

Too Much of a Good Thing

American fans weren't the only ones clamoring for the Beatles. The group had taken over the hit charts in Australia, as well. Eagerly the Aussie fans waited for June to arrive, when the Beatles would be touring "Down Under."

Australian fans proved to be just as wild as their American and British counterparts. But by now, mob scenes had lost their thrill for the Beatles. There was something frightening and abnormal about it all. The Beatles were tired of wearing disguises just to safely cross the street. They were tired of worrying about the safety of their families and homes. They were tired of being smuggled from hotel room to stage to airport.

Most of all, they were tired of not being able to

hear themselves sing.

Ever since they were teenagers practicing in their bedrooms, the Beatles had been striving to improve their music. Ironically, now that they had made it, what they sounded like hardly mattered. The nonstop screaming was so loud that the Beatles couldn't even hear their own voices, let alone one another. Their performances became more and more ragged.

Noise wasn't their only problem on stage. Months earlier, George Harrison had mentioned in an interview that his favorite candy was jelly beans. That little piece of trivia literally rained down on the Beatles every night, as fans persisted in throwing jelly beans—sometimes by the bagful— onto the stage.

A Hard Day's Night

In July 1964, the Beatles experienced a different kind of success with the release of their first film, *A Hard Day's Night*. Filmed between their U.S.

and Australian tours, the movie made fun of their lives as Beatles. Naturally, the film had quite a few mob scenes—and a good dose of British humor as well. Even on the silver screen, the Beatles managed to charm their audience. *A Hard Day's Night*—a saying Ringo was fond of using—won over fans and critics alike.

Although Brian Epstein and the Beatles were all living in London by now, they went to Liverpool for the northern premiere of *A Hard Day's Night*. More than 200,000 Liverpudlians—one out of every four citizens—lined the streets to pay tribute to the hometown boys who had conquered the world.

An album of the same name was soon released, too, along with a single. In no time, both went to the top of charts across the world. What's more, all 13 songs on the album were new, composed during the craziness of their tours.

The Beatles returned to the United States in August, after touring Sweden for the second time. The pace of the U.S. tour was incredible—32 shows in 24 cities in 34 days! Often, the Beatles didn't even know what city they were in.

The crowds were just as frantic for the Beatles as they had been during the group's first visit. In fact, if the fans had been allowed to get near them, the Beatles probably would have been badly hurt—or even killed. Sometimes there were unfortunate victims as it was. In San Francisco, for instance, a woman was beaten and robbed in the hotel where the Beatles were staying. Though dozens of police and security guards heard her screams, they just thought she was an especially loud Beatles fan.

The Beatles felt the uncomfortable burden of their fame in other ways as well. Smiling became more difficult as they shook hands with yet another mayor, or held another child stuck into their arms by an eager mother. Disabled fans were wheeled into their dressing room, where it often seemed the fans were waiting to be healed by the touch of a Beatles' hand.

The weary Beatles didn't know what to make of it all. "None of us has quite grasped what it is all about yet," Ringo once commented to a reporter. "It's washing over our heads like a huge tidal wave."

The Beatles are shown here in a scene from their first film, A Hard Day's Night. *The film—and the album of the same name—was a hit with fans and critics alike.*

CHAPTER 6
THE PRICE OF SUCCESS

"I reckon we could send out four wax dummies of ourselves and that would satisfy the crowds. Beatles concerts are nothing to do with music anymore."

—John Lennon

An Award from Buckingham Palace

On June 12, 1965, Buckingham Palace announced that the Beatles had been awarded the Membership of the Most Excellent Order of the British Empire, referred to by Britons as "MBE." The MBE was a prestigious honor usually granted to important war veterans, so the Beatles were surprised when they heard the news. They figured they were being honored for all the money they were bringing into the country!

Former MBE recipients weren't so amused. Many of them, outraged that the award had been granted to mere pop stars, returned their medals in a huff. One of them publicly referred to the Beatles as "vulgar nincompoops."

Despite the controversy, the Beatles did receive their awards—and were even introduced to the queen. "She was just like a mum to us," Paul told reporters later.

Glad to get out of the country for a while, the Beatles next went on tour in France, Italy, and

Spain. Surprisingly, their concerts weren't always sellouts. Maybe the European fans had gotten tired of listening to screams instead of music.

American fans weren't at that point yet. When the Beatles played New York City's Shea Stadium in August 1965, nearly 56,000 people swarmed into the massive stadium to "hear" the Beatles sing. That set a new world record for a pop concert. Even the Beatles got caught up in the excitement. For one concert, anyway, the old spark was back.

In general, though, the constant noise and confusion were quickly wearing them down. Tense and frustrated, they would sometimes stop playing in the middle of songs. Sometimes John Lennon would swear at the unknowing crowd.

Fortunately, there was still one outlet for their musical creativity: the recording studio. After a short tour of Britain in September—it would be their last British tour—they spent four calm weeks in the Abbey Road studios. There the Beatles put their energy into making better music. The result was their *Rubber Soul* album, released in early December. It was their most ambitious project yet.

Crossed Signals
In Manila

In 1966, the Beatles didn't make any live appearances until early summer. Then all the madness began again. "I reckon we could send out four wax dummies of ourselves and that would satisfy the crowds," said a cynical John Lennon. "Beatles concerts are nothing to do with music any more."

First, the Beatles toured West Germany, including their old stomping grounds, Hamburg. From there they went on to Tokyo, Japan, where they were booked for three days at the Nippon Budokan. This eight-sided hall was considered by many Japanese to be sacred. In fact, many people thought that the Nippon Budokan should be used only for traditional Japanese martial arts. Some of them marched outside the hall, protesting the Beatles' performances there.

Events took a turn for the worse at the Beatles' next stop, the Philippines.

The day before their concerts, the *Manila*

Sunday Times reported that First Lady Imelda Marcos had invited the Beatles to a garden party. Besides the usual dignitaries, 300 children—mostly war orphans and the disabled—were invited as well.

But the Beatles didn't know anything about the fancy event. When the time came for the July 4 party, they were sleeping in their hotel. That afternoon and evening, they gave two concerts before a total of 80,000 cheering Filipinos.

The very next morning, all good feelings toward the Beatles were forgotten. **"Imelda Stood Up!"** screamed a bold headline in the *Manila Times*. The Filipinos, thinking their first lady had been purposely insulted, were quick to react. Bomb and death threats were phoned to the Beatles' hotel and to the British Embassy.

Trying to calm the situation, Brian Epstein hired a television crew to tape an official apology. But when the segment aired, there was so much static that Brian's words couldn't be understood at all. Mysteriously, the static vanished as soon as Brian stopped speaking.

At that point, the Beatles wanted nothing so much as to get out of there. It would be rough going. Police protection for the Beatles was withdrawn as soon as news of the incident came out. The concert promoter refused to pay them for their two successful concerts, even as tax authorities hounded them to pay up.

"Beatles Go Home!" chanted 200 angry Filipinos at the Manila airport. Running for their lives, the Beatles managed to board their plane without serious injury. Other members of their team weren't as fortunate. Brian Epstein sprained his ankle when he was kicked and thrown to the ground. The assistant road manager, Mal Evans, suffered bruised ribs. The chauffeur was dealt a spinal injury and a fractured rib.

In a bit of ironic timing, a press statement from President Marcos was issued just minutes after the Beatles' plane finally took off. "There was no intention on the part of the Beatles to slight the First Lady or the Government of the Republic of the Philippines," it read.

Backlash!

After their unsettling experience in Manila, the Beatles spent a short time in New Delhi, India. Then they headed back home. At the London airport, a reporter asked George Harrison what was next on the Beatles' schedule. "We're going to have a couple of weeks to recuperate before we go and get beaten up by the Americans," George replied, somewhat bitterly.

His prediction wasn't far off.

Months earlier, John Lennon had been interviewed by Maureen Cleave for the *London Evening Standard*. In the interview, John expressed his views on the role of religion in modern society. "Christianity will go. It will vanish and shrink. I needn't argue about that. I'm right and I will be proved right. We're more popular than Jesus now," John said.

In England, no one batted an eye when they read that statement. Most people understood what John meant—that in day-to-day living, organized religion was becoming less important to people.

That was no criticism of religion or of Jesus. It was just a fact, a social trend.

The trouble started when that interview got into the wrong hands. *Datebook*, an American teen magazine, reprinted the article in its July 29, 1966 issue. John Lennon's comments were blown all out of proportion. "Lennon Claims Beatles are Bigger than Jesus Christ!" cried the headline. People assumed that John meant the Beatles were **greater** than Jesus.

The backlash against the bewildered group was almost immediate. Former fans turned into sworn enemies as dozens of radio stations banned the playing of Beatles music. Some stations even sponsored public burnings of Beatles records and merchandise. Record stores refused to sell the group's records. Church ministers preached long sermons against the evils of rock 'n' roll. Some even threatened to revoke church membership of anyone who went to see the group perform.

The Beatles were scheduled to start their U.S. tour in Chicago on August 12. That very day, they held a press conference to try to set the record straight. Upstairs in his hotel room just before the conference, John Lennon broke down and cried under the pressure. Then he went down and faced the reporters and television cameras.

"I'm not anti-God, anti-Christ or anti-religion," he told them. "I was not saying we are greater or better...I'm sorry I said it, really. I never meant it to be a lousy anti-religion thing. From what I've read, or observed, Christianity just seems to me to be shrinking, to be losing contact."

Later, he explained that what bothered him the most about the whole situation was the physical burning of the records. "I couldn't go away knowing that I created another little place of hate in the world," he stated. "Especially with something as uncomplicated as people listening to records and dancing and playing and enjoying what the Beatles are."

From there, the tour went on as scheduled. There was no joy left in performing, however. Worried about being shot by a sniper, receiving hate mail all the while, the tour was a nightmare for all of them. When a firecracker exploded onstage at the Memphis Coliseum, George Harrison nearly fainted with fright. Paul got so nervous before a rainy Cincinatti performance that he threw up backstage.

Of course, the controversy hadn't affected all of their followers. Screaming, hysterical fans still followed their every move—but the numbers were decreasing. A year earlier, when the Beatles played Shea Stadium, they had broken the world record. This time there were 11,000 empty seats.

On August 29, 1966, the Beatles performed at Candlestick Park in San Francisco. It was to be their last public concert.

CHAPTER 7: SIGN OF THE TIMES

"For me, it was the most innovative, imaginative and trend-setting record of its time."

—George Martin on *Sergeant Pepper*

Sergeant Pepper's Lonely Hearts Club Band

Although their fans might not have wanted to admit it, the Beatles were well beyond the "adorable mop-top" stage. Three out of the four Beatles were now married, and two of them had children. Ringo had married a Liverpool hairdresser, Maureen Cox, in February 1965. They had a son named Zak. George and model Patti Boyd were married in January 1966. John and Cynthia's son, Julian, would be starting school in a couple of years. Paul was the only unmarried Beatle, and even he was involved in a long-term relationship with actress Jane Asher.

If the Beatles had been in the music business just for fame and fortune, they could easily have retired after their last concert. But good music was more important to them than that. Their fans might have been content with simple, catchy love songs, but the Beatles weren't.

This attitude came through on their album

Revolver, released shortly before the American tour. The songs included "Eleanor Rigby," "Yellow Submarine," "Got to Get You Into My Life," and "Taxman," which was George Harrison's first big hit. Besides being more complex musically, the Beatles also touched on themes such as loneliness and political satire. Most of all, they proved that an entire LP—not just individual songs—could be a creative medium, like a painter's canvas.

The Beatles took this idea even further with their next album, *Sergeant Pepper's Lonely Hearts Club Band*. In the album, the Beatles "pretended" to be another band. Musically, each song sounded quite different from the others. At the same time, there were no breaks between songs, which made it sound like a live performance. *Sergeant Pepper* was also the first album to include printed lyrics of each song.

Besides the title song, other songs included "With a Little Help From My Friends," "Fixing a Hole," and "Being for the Benefit of Mr. Kite!" The final song, "A Day in the Life," ended with a crescendo by a 41-piece symphony orchestra. At the very end was a note so high that only dogs could hear it!

Sergeant Pepper's Lonely Hearts Club Band was a very difficult project. While the Beatles' first album, *Please Please Me,* took less than 10 hours to record, *Sergeant Pepper* was 700 hours in the making! "I remember it warmly, as both a tremendous challenge and a highly rewarding experience," recalled producer George Martin. "For me, it was the most innovative, imaginative, and trend-setting record of its time."

Influencing the album—at least in part—was the Beatles' recent interest in the drug LSD. Ever since their intense days in Hamburg, the Beatles had often used drugs to give them energy or to help them relax. Now, however, they began to think that drugs might be a key to "expanded consciousness."

On an LSD "trip," people perceive such things as color and sound in new ways. Sometimes they see or feel things that aren't there. The Beatles were by no means the only ones experimenting with the drug. In fact, LSD, often called "acid," was still legal in Great Britain when the Beatles started taking it.

As soon as the album came out in the spring of 1967, fans and critics alike pointed out all the phrases that seemingly were references to drugs. For example, "Lucy in the Sky With Diamonds" was thought to stand for LSD. John, however, insisted that he had gotten the idea for the song from a drawing his son Julian had made.

The Beatles soon got annoyed by all the people trying to find hidden meanings. Even so, *Sergeant Pepper* was quickly adopted as a cultural symbol of the late 1960's.

In the midst of the drug uproar, the Beatles experienced yet another high point in their career. They took part in one of the first satellite television programs, which included segments from different nations. On June 25, 1967, nearly 200 million people watched as the Beatles sang "All You Need Is Love" at their studios on Abbey Road.

A Little Peace of Mind

One by one, the Beatles came to the conclusion that drugs were not the answer. Their search for self-awareness and contentment went on, however. Like many others at the time, the Beatles found themselves drawn to Eastern religions. Variations of Hinduism and Buddhism were becoming more and more accepted in the Western world. People were especially interested in the practice of meditation.

On August 24, George's wife, Patti, convinced the Beatles to attend a lecture by the Maharishi Mahesh Yogi. The Maharishi had founded the Spiritual Regeneration Movement. The Beatles were impressed with the lecture. Although none of them was involved with organized religion, they were all very interested in spiritual growth. The Maharishi's talk of "inner peace" was soothing to them.

The very next day, the Beatles and their wives followed the Maharishi to the University College in Bangor, North Wales. There they were to take part in a 10-day instructional course, along with many others.

The Beatles had studied with the Maharishi only a short time when they received some shocking news. Their manager, Brian Epstein, was dead.

Brian—a celebrity himself—had taken an overdose of sleeping pills. Because the pills had been taken over a period of days rather than all at once, no one knew if his death was an accident or a suicide. According to his friends, however, Brian had been depressed for some time and had been abusing both alcohol and drugs.

The man who gave the world the Beatles was buried quietly in Liverpool.

Magical Mystery Tour

Soon after Brian's death, the Beatles regrouped to start work on their next project, a film and album called *Magical Mystery Tour*. The idea behind it was simple: the Beatles, a camera crew, and a "cast"—including circus fat ladies and midgets—would drive across the country, filming whatever happened. There would be no script, no rehearsals, and no director.

The problem was that nothing very interesting happened to the 43 people assembled in the brightly painted tour bus. No amount of editing could change that fact. Rather than scrap the whole project, however, the Beatles released it as planned.

Magical Mystery Tour was shown on television in Great Britain the day after Christmas 1967. Nearly 15 million people tuned in—but even the most devoted fans couldn't find much good to say about it. The press, usually kind to the Beatles, didn't hesitate to pan them. "Blatant rubbish!" exclaimed one critic.

Because the whole thing had been mostly Paul's idea, he felt he owed the public an apology. "It was like getting a bash in the face," he admitted to reporters. "We goofed, really."

The Beatles might not have been successful filmmakers, but they could still make great music. In the United States, *Magical Mystery Tour*—the album—made $8 million in the first 10 days. Besides the title song, it contained the hits "Fool on the Hill" and "I Am the Walrus."

Beautiful Places

At this point, the Beatles had to deal with a problem few people ever face—too much money. On the advice of their financial consultants, the Beatles started investing their wealth in business interests. In December 1967, they opened the Apple Boutique in London. As Paul McCartney announced to the press, the boutique was "a beautiful place where you can buy beautiful things." Because the Beatles and the people they hired to run the place were so casual about its operation, the boutique was also a shoplifter's heaven. It started losing money from the first day!

In the offices above the boutique, however, a new "empire" was born. Apple Corps., Ltd., was formed in January 1968. Besides the boutique, its divisions included Apple Records, Apple Films, and Apple Publishing. Later, they added the Apple

Foundation for the Arts, which promised large grants of money to people with a creative spark. Idealistic as always, the Beatles didn't foresee the flood of requests that would come from talented and untalented people alike.

Even with all that was going on in their lives, the Beatles hadn't forgotten the Maharishi. In February 1968, they went with their wives to Rishikesh, India, for a three-month religious retreat. Other people attended the retreat as well.

As the Ganges River flowed gently by, the Beatles dedicated themselves to a calm life of fasting, meditation, and mass prayer. They found it easy to write new songs in this atmosphere. Most of their evenings were spent singing and strumming their guitars.

Peaceful as the setting was, however, not all the Beatles were comfortable with this lifestyle. Ringo soon decided that it wasn't for him. He left after a couple of weeks, and was soon followed by Paul.

Only George and John remained committed to the Maharishi. Soon, even they had their faith shaken. They'd heard that the Maharishi was using the Beatles to draw attention to his group. Another rumor, despite all his talk about spirituality, was that the Maharishi was having an affair with one of the women followers. Disappointed again, the two remaining Beatles turned their back on him as well.

Growing Tension

The Beatles' next project was the film *Yellow Submarine*, a cartoon film based on a song from *Revolver*. Distracted by their business dealings, the Beatles weren't really in the mood for a new project. Halfheartedly, they recorded several new songs—and for the first time, gave their public less than their best work.

Their lack of enthusiasm didn't come across in the film, however. *Yellow Submarine* was released in London on July 17, 1968. It didn't get good reviews, but people seemed to enjoy the film. They thought the little mustached cartoon figures of the Beatles were a lot of fun.

After the Beatles finished working on *Yellow Submarine*, they began recording a double-album set called simply *The Beatles*. Because of its plain white jacket, it was known as the *White* album. The set contained 30 songs, including "Ob-La-Di, Ob-La-Da," "While My Guitar Gently Weeps," "Revolution," and "Helter Skelter." Five months were spent recording and mixing tracks before the Beatles were satisfied with their work.

Although the *White* album was well received, it marked a turning point for the Beatles. They were growing apart, both personally and musically. Despite having succeeded as a group, they all felt overlooked as individuals. Frustrations that had been there since they were teenagers now grew more intense.

As John grew more rebellious, Paul became more demanding. George, a gifted songwriter in his own right, felt slighted. Ringo wondered if the group even needed him anymore.

Let It Be

Tensions mounted as the Beatles' personal lives became more complicated. John Lennon's marriage ended when he became involved with an avant-gard artist, Yoko Ono. For Cynthia, who had been with him since his Quarry Men days, it was like getting a divorce from her friends as well.

Paul McCartney sensed how she was feeling. One day, carrying a red rose, he drove out to see Cynthia and five-year-old Julian. During the drive, he made up a song to cheer the little boy. That song turned into "Hey Jude," one of the best-loved of all the Beatles' songs.

In the meantime, the Beatles weren't adjusting well to John's new situation. John and Yoko were always together—even during recording sessions. What's more, John was beginning to break out of the "Beatle role" he'd felt confined by for so long. The small Japanese-American woman seemed to give John courage.

Together, John and Yoko gave art exhibits no one understood. They made experimental films, and also recorded albums of experimental music. Their first album, *Unfinished Music No. 1: Two Virgins*, got more attention for its record jacket than the music itself. It showed John and Yoko naked and holding hands in a messy apartment.

Most people didn't react very well to the "new" John Lennon. But by now, John was past the point of caring. "I suppose I've spoiled my image," John explained impatiently to a reporter. "[People] just want me to be lovable. But I was never that."

As the Beatles grew farther apart, Paul McCartney began to regret their decision not to tour anymore. Maybe what the group needed was to play before live audiences again—to sing to real people instead of to recording equipment. Maybe if the Beatles got back to their musical roots, they would get back on track again. But the other Beatles weren't at all interested in turning back the clock.

Instead of live touring, the Beatles began work on a documentary film in January 1969. It showed the Beatles at work on another album, originally called *Get Back*. The name was later changed to *Let It Be*. It was not a happy time for any of them.

For months, the tapes for the *Let It Be* film and music sat in the studio, unedited. "No one could look at them," admitted John Lennon. Finally, a famous rock producer, Phil Spector, was hired to put the album together. The Beatles weren't happy with the results, however, nor were the critics. Today, *Let It Be* is usually regarded as the Beatles' least memorable album.

To many people, the Beatles and their music were a symbol of the 1960's.

CHAPTER 8
SEPARATE LIVES

"I'd like to say thank you very much on behalf of the group and myself and I hope we passed the audition."

—John Lennon in the film, *Let It Be*

A New Decade

On March 12, 1969, Paul McCartney married rock photographer Linda Eastman—and broke the hearts of young women all over the world. Just eight days later, John Lennon and Yoko Ono were married in Gibraltar. Instead of a honeymoon, John and Yoko staged a "bed-in" in protest of the Vietnam War. For several days, they just sat in an Amsterdam hotel bed, holding flowers and talking with journalists about peace.

Before the 1960's came to a close, the Beatles managed one last masterpiece. July and August 1969 were spent at the Abbey Road studios. It was almost like old times. Putting aside their differences, they recorded the album *Abbey Road*. The songs included "Octopus's Garden," "Here Comes the Sun," "Something," and "Mean Mr. Mustard."

Released in early fall, many of the songs on *Abbey Road* were considered some of the Beatles' best work. More than five million copies were sold that year—outselling even *Sergeant Pepper*.

In October, an American radio announcer got an anonymous phone call saying that Paul McCartney was dead. The "proof," said the caller, could be found in John's "Strawberry Fields," from *Magical Mystery Tour*. When played backwards, the end of the song sounded like "I buried Paul," he said.

That was all it took to start a storm of wild theories and explanations. Though he knew about the rumor, Paul didn't respond to it—which didn't help the situation. Paul was at his Scottish farm with his family, and was determined to protect their privacy. Finally, some persistent *Life* magazine reporters managed to track him down and set the record straight.

The fans were wrong. Paul was not dead. The Beatles were.

In March 1970, Paul returned to London with his first solo album in hand, simply called *McCartney*. A few weeks later, he announced to the stunned world that he was leaving the Beatles "because of personal, business, and musical differences." The only Beatle who had never threatened to quit was now the one to formally end the group.

The next month, the Beatles' film, *Let It Be,* premiered at the London Palladium. The last scene showed the Beatles performing on a cold winter day on the rooftop of their Apple studios.

At the very end comes John Lennon's voice: "I'd like to say thank you very much on behalf of the group and myself and I hope we passed the audition."

After the Beatles

The Beatles were no more, but George, Paul, John, and Ringo went on with their lives. In the years after the breakup, most of their bad feelings were put aside. After all, their friendship was very special. Only another ex-Beatle could know what it was like for a young Liverpool skiffle player to make it to the top.

Musicians as they were, they each continued recording albums. Many of the albums were very successful. Some were not.

The men have made their mark in other ways as well. In 1971, George Harrison organized a benefit concert for famine relief in Bangladesh. The benefit is often considered the forerunner of such events as Band Aid and Live Aid.

Ringo, continuing a trend from his Beatle days, has appeared in many movies. In 1985 he became the first Beatle to become a grandparent. Recently, he and his second wife, actress Barbara Bach, worked with a children's television program on public television.

Paul's interests have remained his family and his music. He and his band, Wings, have produced many hits. In fact, Paul McCartney went down in the *Guinness Book of World Records* as being the first person to sell 100 million albums and 100 million singles.

From 1975 to 1980, John Lennon quietly took care of his young son, Sean, while Yoko managed their business deals. Then, in late fall of 1980, he and Yoko released the well-received album, *Double Fantasy*. It would be 40-year-old John Lennon's last album.

Just before 11 p.m. on December 8, 1980, John and Yoko were returning to their apartment in New York City. As they entered the Dakota, a voice called out John's name. John turned around, expecting an autograph seeker. Before he could say a word, a mentally disturbed fan named Mark David Chapman shot him several times in the chest. John Lennon died soon afterwards.

The entire world grieved for the man whose songs, played loud among friends or on headphones late at night, had touched the spirit of a generation.

So many years later, those songs still go on.

Though the Beatles broke up in 1970, the four boys from Liverpool —and their music—will never be forgotten.

GLOSSARY

acetate—the material out of which records are made.
avant-garde—having to do with new, experimental ideas in arts such as writing, painting, sculpture, etc.
charismatic—having a very special charm or appeal.
chords—three or more musical notes played together to make a harmony.
condensation—steam that is cooled to form water.
country music—American music that developed from the folk style of the rural South.
crescendo—a musical term that means to grow steadily louder.
cultural—having to do with the beliefs, values, artistic expressions, and behavior of a group of people in a given time.
demo tape—"demonstration" tape. Musicians make demo tapes to interest recording companies in their songs.
documentary—a film that presents factual information about a person or event.
editing—to make a final version of a movie or record by cutting or rearranging the film or tape.
folk music—simple songs that are traditional among the people of a particular region. The songs often reflect the peoples' lifestyles and concerns.
innovative—to do something in a new, clever way.
jazz—American music that uses rhythmic variations, improvisation and complicated melodies.
kazoo—a small, inexpensive instrument that "buzzes" when it is blown into.
LP—a long-playing phonograph record, designed to be played at 33 1/3 revolutions, or turns, per minute.

GLOSSARY

LSD—the drug lysergic acid diethylamide.
lyrics—the words to a song.
manager—a person who conducts business affairs on the behalf of others.
meditation—in a religious sense, to focus one's thoughts for a period of time in order to achieve calmness and inner peace.
record label, recording label—the name of a company or division that puts out a record.
recuperate—to get back to normal after a difficult experience.
rhythm & blues—black American vocal music, usually used for dancing.
rock 'n' roll—popular music that has a strong beat and usually includes electronic instruments, such as the electric guitar.
single—a record featuring one song, with another song on the flip side.
skiffle—simple jazz or folk music played with at least some nonstandard instruments.
sniper—a person who shoots someone, usually from a hidden place.
stage presence—a special quality of a performer that allows him or her to hold the attention of an audience.
teddy boy—British slang for a violent young "thug" who dresses in a certain style.
tune—to adjust the musical pitch of an instrument.
ventilation—the flow of air through a room or building.
yogi—a mystical religious teacher who practices Hindu philosophy.

INDEX

Abbey Road Studios 52, 77, 89, 102
albums 6, 56, 72, 77, 86-89, 93, 95-96, 98-99, 102
Best, Pete 36, 38-39, 52-53
Casbah Coffee Club 29-30, 36, 39
Cavern Club 35, 41-45, 48, 53, 63
"Ed Sullivan Show" 69
EMI 51-52, 66
Epstein, Brian 35, 42-44, 48-49, 51, 53-54, 72, 79-80, 91
films 71-72, 91-92, 95-99
Hamburg, W. Germany 36-40, 49, 69, 78, 88
Harrison, George 6-8, 18-19, 26, 27, 36-39, 64, 71, 81, 84, 86-87, 90, 94, 96, 104-105
Kirchherr, Astrid 40, 49
Lennon, Cynthia (Powell) 53, 62-63, 86, 92
Lennon, John 6-11, 13-16, 20, 23-30, 33, 36, 38, 44, 53, 55, 62-64, 75-78, 81-83, 86, 89, 94, 96-106
Lennon, Julia 14, 27-29, 86
Lennon, Julian 62-63, 89, 97
LSD 88-89
Maharishi 90-91, 94-95
Martin, George 47, 51-52, 54-55, 85, 88
McCartney, Paul 6-8, 17-19, 23-28, 36, 38-40, 54, 64, 68, 76, 84, 86, 92-94, 96-98, 102-105
Ono, Yoko 97-98, 102, 105-106
Quarry Men 16, 23-32, 97
skiffle 13, 15-16, 20-21, 24, 26, 39, 104
songs 6-7, 10, 41, 43, 47-48, 54-56, 66-69, 72, 87-89, 93, 96, 102-103
Starr, Ringo (Richard Starkey) 6-8, 19-21, 37, 52-53, 61, 64, 68, 72-73, 86, 94, 96, 104-105
Sutcliffe, Stuart 30-33, 36, 38, 40, 49-50
Top Ten Club 38, 39, 41
Williams, Allan 31, 32, 36

LISTENING CHOICES

Songs

"A Day in the Life"
"All You Need Is Love"
"Back in the U.S.S.R."
"Come Together"
"Dear Prudence"
"Eleanor Rigby"
"Helter Skelter"
"Hey Jude"
"I am the Walrus"
"Julia"
"Lady Madonna"
"The Long and Winding Road"
"Love Me Do"
"Lucy In the Sky With Diamonds"
"Norwegian Wood"
"Nowhere Man"
"Octopus's Garden"
"Penny Lane"
"Please Please Me"
"Revolution"
"She Loves You"
"Strawberry Fields"
"While My Guitar Gently Weeps"
"With a Little Help From My Friends"
"Yesterday"

Albums

Please Please Me
Meet the Beatles
A Hard Day's Night
Beatles for Sale
Help!
Rubber Soul
Revolver
Sergeant Pepper's Lonely Hearts Club Band
Magical Mystery Tour
The Beatles (The *White Album*)
Abbey Road
Let It Be

Films

A Hard Day's Night
Help!
Magical Mystery Tour
Yellow Submarine
Let It Be (documentary)